# Inside the Tomb of TUTANKHAMUN

First American edition published in 2005 by
Enchanted Lion Books
115 West 18 Street, 6th floor
New York, NY 10011

ISBN 1-59270-042-X

Catalog-in-Publishing Data is on file with the Library of Congress

*Author:*
**Jacqueline Morley** studied English at Oxford University. She has taught
English and History and has a special interest in the history of everyday life.
She has written historical fiction and non-fiction for children and is the author
of the prizewinning **An Egyptian Pyramid.**

*Artist:*
**John James** was born in London in 1959. He studied at Eastbourne College
of Art and has specialized in historical reconstruction since leaving school in
1982. He now lives in Sussex.

*Series Creator:*
**David Salariya** was born in Dundee, Scotland. He has illustrated a wide
range of books and has created and designed many new series for publishers
both in the UK and overseas. In 1989, he established The Salariya Book
Company. He lives in Brighton with his wife, illustrator Shirley Willis, and their
son Jonathan.

*Editor:* **Penny Clarke**

Due to the changing nature of internet links, the following
online list of websites related to the subject of this book, has been developed.
This site is updated regularly. Please use this link to access the list:
**http://www.book-house.co.uk/inside/tut**

Printed and bound in China. Printed on paper from sustainable forests.

Photographic credits
t=top b=bottom c=center l=left r=right

The Art Archive / Dagli Orti: 18, 19, 20, 34, 35t, 43
The Art Archive / Domenica del Corriere/ Dagli Orti: 23
The Art Archive / Egyptian Museum Cairo: 31r
The Art Archive / Egyptian Museum Cairo / Dagli Orti (A): 14, 16, 37b, 40, 41
The Art Archive / Egyptian Museum Turin / Dagli Orti (A): 11
Griffith Institute, Oxford: 24, 25, 25, 27, 29, 31b, 35b, 37t, 38, 39, 42

Every effort has been made to trace copyright holders. The Salariya Book Company apologizes for any
unintentional omissions and would be pleased, in such cases, to add an acknowledgment in future editions.

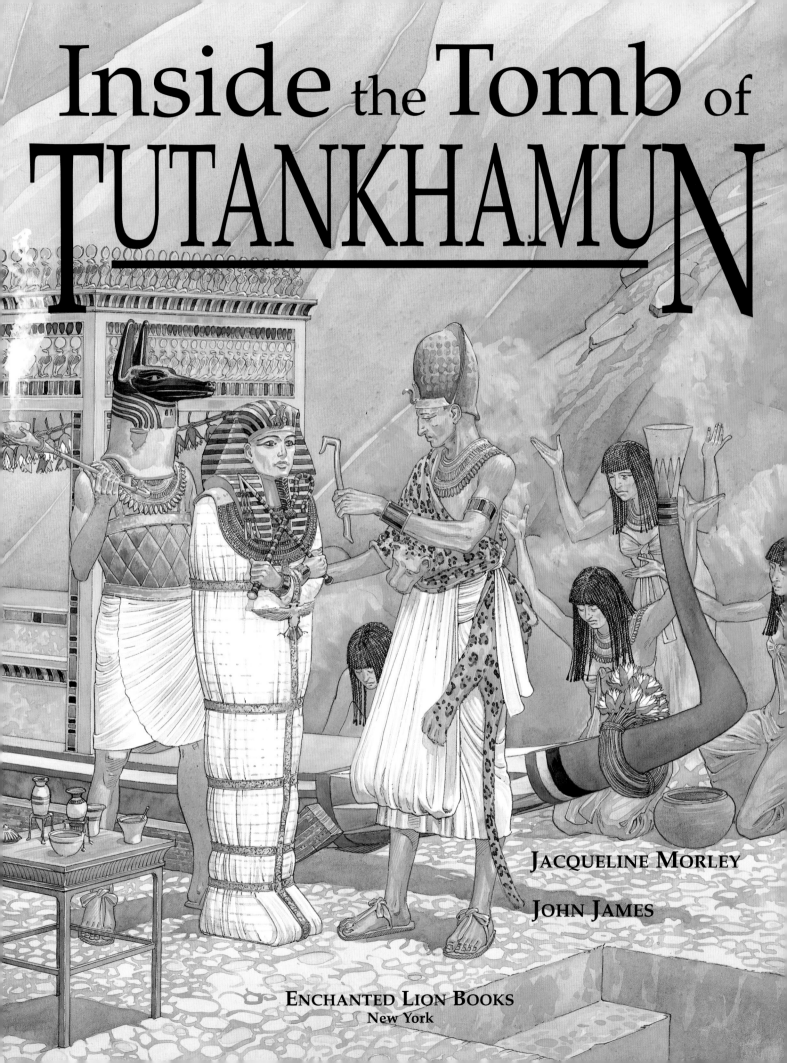

# Inside the Tomb of
# TUTANKHAMUN

JACQUELINE MORLEY

JOHN JAMES

ENCHANTED LION BOOKS
New York

# CONTENTS

# INTRODUCTION

This story takes you to the ancient kingdom of Egypt. Kings had ruled there since before 3000 BCE. The ancient Egyptian term for "king" was "pharaoh." The pharaohs of Egypt had great power, for their people believed them to be gods on earth. In 1333 BCE a boy aged about nine became pharaoh, but he did not rule for long. Today, however, he is the most famous of all the pharaohs. Many people who know nothing else about ancient Egyptian history know his name.

So how did a pharaoh who was unimportant in his lifetime become so famous? The answer is because of a great archaeological discovery.

Archaeologists do detective work about the past, examining things that have survived from long ago. These are usually so broken, trampled, overgrown or built over that they are just fragments deep in the ground. Digging them out and piecing them together is slow, painstaking work that never makes the headlines. But, just once in a while, an archaeologist finds something so amazing that the whole world wants to know about it. That's how it was with the tomb of pharaoh Tutankhamun.

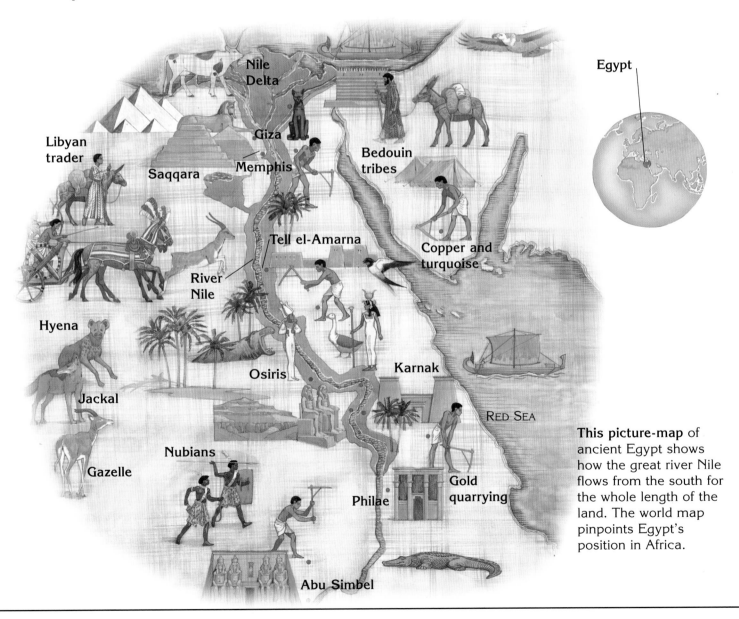

**This picture-map** of ancient Egypt shows how the great river Nile flows from the south for the whole length of the land. The world map pinpoints Egypt's position in Africa.

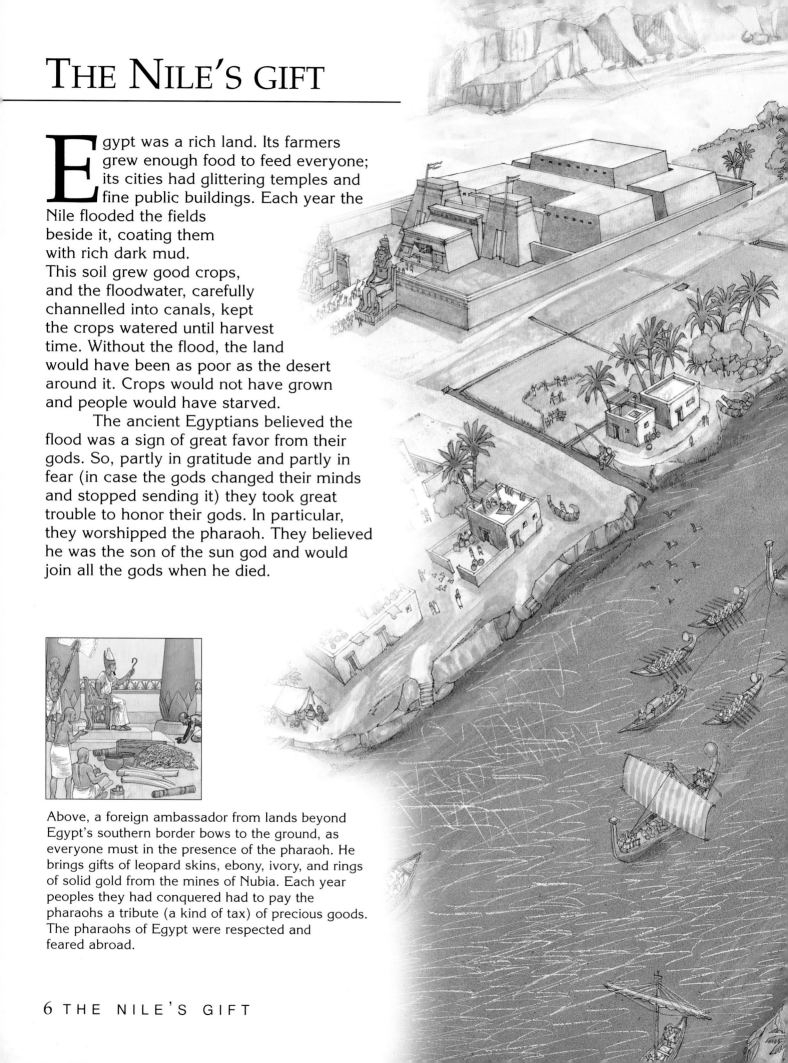

# THE NILE'S GIFT

Egypt was a rich land. Its farmers grew enough food to feed everyone; its cities had glittering temples and fine public buildings. Each year the Nile flooded the fields beside it, coating them with rich dark mud. This soil grew good crops, and the floodwater, carefully channelled into canals, kept the crops watered until harvest time. Without the flood, the land would have been as poor as the desert around it. Crops would not have grown and people would have starved.

The ancient Egyptians believed the flood was a sign of great favor from their gods. So, partly in gratitude and partly in fear (in case the gods changed their minds and stopped sending it) they took great trouble to honor their gods. In particular, they worshipped the pharaoh. They believed he was the son of the sun god and would join all the gods when he died.

Above, a foreign ambassador from lands beyond Egypt's southern border bows to the ground, as everyone must in the presence of the pharaoh. He brings gifts of leopard skins, ebony, ivory, and rings of solid gold from the mines of Nubia. Each year peoples they had conquered had to pay the pharaohs a tribute (a kind of tax) of precious goods. The pharaohs of Egypt were respected and feared abroad.

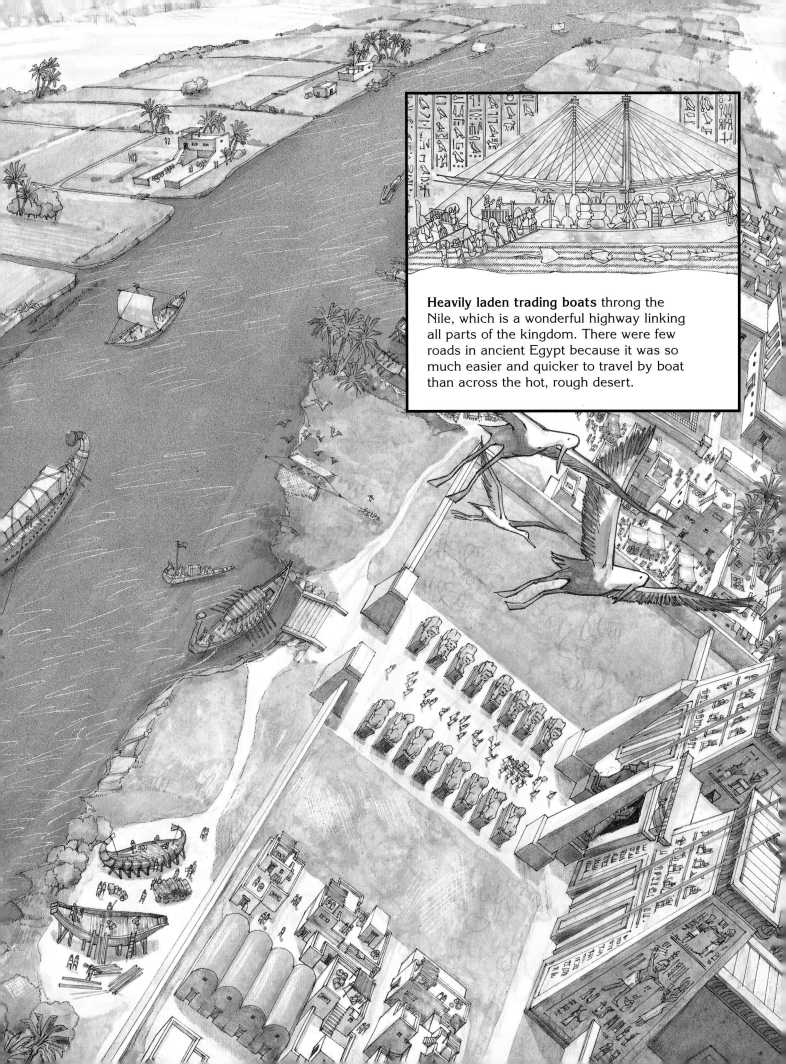

**Heavily laden trading boats** throng the Nile, which is a wonderful highway linking all parts of the kingdom. There were few roads in ancient Egypt because it was so much easier and quicker to travel by boat than across the hot, rough desert.

# THE PHARAOH AND HIS PEOPLE

A pharaoh had huge power. He owned everything, knew everything and decided everything. Or, at least, everyone acted as if he did. In fact, Egypt was run by large numbers of officials. They sent reports to their ministers detailing everything they did, and these ministers reported to the pharaoh who then made his all-wise decisions. Since every pharaoh was head of the law courts and the treasury, commander of the army and chief priest, a strong pharaoh really did have total power, but a young or weak one could find that his officials were controlling him.

The pharaoh lived in luxury, and so did his ministers. They had big town houses and large country estates. Most townsfolk made a living supplying the rich with goods. Fine craftsmen were well paid and anyone with a trade could find work. Yet most people were very poor. These were the people who worked the land and kept everyone else fed. Most had only a patch of land of their own. In return for using it they had to spend most of their time farming the estate of their rich landlord.

**Craftsmen** finishing a gilded shrine

Potter

Government scribe

**The pharaoh** had two chief ministers, called viziers, one for Upper Egypt and one for Lower Egypt. They kept an eye on all the departments of government.

**Hundreds of craftsmen** worked for the pharaoh, making beautiful objects for him to use in this life and in his life after death.

**Even though their pharaoh** is not expected to die for years, these painters are already busy on his tomb. You'll read why later.

**Many Egyptians** could not read and write. If they had to send a letter they paid a scribe (a professional writer) to write it. Government scribes wrote the records of all official business.

Attendant and fan bearer

General receiving orders

Enslaving captured foes

Bargaining at the market

Farm laborers

Scribe, a professional letter writer

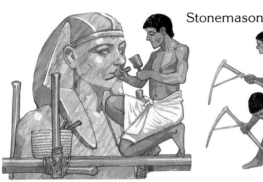
Stonemason

**The pharaoh's** realm was so strung out along the Nile that it was split into several regions, or provinces, so it could be run efficiently. Each province had a governor.

**Taxmen** were unpopular officials. Every year they checked what each farmer was growing and told him how much of his harvest he would have to pay to the pharaoh.

The pharaoh and his queen

**Every town** had at least one temple. On the day of a god's festival its image was taken from the temple and paraded through the streets for people to worship. It was carried in a covered shrine, as only priests could look at the sacred image. People believed that the god was there in its image and that the temple was its home. Each day priests washed and dressed it and offered it food. Ordinary people placed offerings on altars in the temple forecourt but were not allowed in the temple.

**The priests'** rituals were too sacred for ordinary people to see, though specially chosen women dancers performed sacred dances at some ceremonies.

High priest

Temple dancer

# PHARAOH THE GOD

To the ancient Egyptians the pharaoh was a son of Re, the sun god. When he died, the pharaoh travelled to the land of the dead in the west, where the sun sets. Each day he would be reborn with the sun, crossing the sky in the sun's boat, so ensuring his people would always enjoy the gods' blessing. But to join the gods the pharaoh's spirit had to stay alive after his death, which meant that his body had to be preserved. So the dead pharaoh was embalmed and carefully wrapped (a process called mummification) and placed in a tomb to preserve him forever. Everything he would need in the next life was buried with him: fine cloth, food, furniture, weapons, and precious objects made of gold and encrusted with jewels.

The first pharaohs were buried in pyramids, huge stone monuments to protect the tomb hidden inside. But however cleverly a pyramid's entrance was concealed, robbers eventually found a way in, ransacked the tomb and stole its treasures.

**The first pyramids** were built of stone blocks, in layers of decreasing size, and topped with a pointed capstone. The stepped sides were then trimmed smooth. Later pyramids were made of mud-brick and have mostly crumbled away.

**Some ancient Egyptian gods**: 1) Hathor 2) Horus 3) Isis 4) Maat 5) Amun 6) Khons 7) Harakhty and 8) Osiris. Their strange heads and head-dresses are symbols expressing each god's particular powers.

**Thousands of laborers** worked for many years to build a pyramid. Huge blocks of stone, ferried from the quarries, were dragged up ramps and set in position with great accuracy.

Pyramids were obvious targets for thieves. The pharaohs of the New Kingdom (1567-1085 BCE) tried to protect their tombs by making them more difficult to find. Instead of building upwards they ordered that their tombs be tunnelled into the rocky slopes of a well-hidden valley in hills to the west of the Nile, thereby creating passages and chambers in the hillside.

Deep pit

Burial chamber

Storeroom

**The cutaway shows** a typical rock-cut tomb. A passage and several stairways lead down to the burial chamber and storerooms.

To baffle thieves and guard against flooding, a deep pit was cut in the floor of the passage, near the entrance.

**Left, a statue of Amun,** the god of the wind, protects the young pharaoh Tutankhamun who stands at his side.

**Above, Shu, the god of the air,** lifted up his daughter, the goddess Nut, to form the sky, separating her from Geb, the earth.

# THE WEALTH OF AMUN

The most magnificent buildings in any Egyptian city were its temples. Everything else, even the pharaoh's own palace, was built of mud-bricks, but the homes of the gods were made of stone, so they would last forever. In New Kingdom times the most important temple was the great temple of Amun at Thebes. Amun had always been important in that region – he was the city's protector god – but when the New Kingdom pharaohs decided to make Thebes their capital, the worship of Amun spread throughout the whole of Egypt. It suited the people of Thebes to claim that he was the greatest of all the gods. They joined his name to that of the sun god and called him Amun-Re.

**The ancient Egyptians** had no money (it had not been invented). People used cloth, grain, oil, wine and other useful things to pay for what they wanted. Amun's farms and workshops produced large quantities of these things. In theory they belonged to the god, but it was the priests who used them. This made the high priest of the cult of Amun a very rich and influential person.

**New Kingdom temples** had magnificent gateways flanked by pylons with gilded flag-poles. This one has a processional way lined with statues of lions. Brightly painted wall carvings show the pharaoh crushing his enemies or making offerings to the gods.

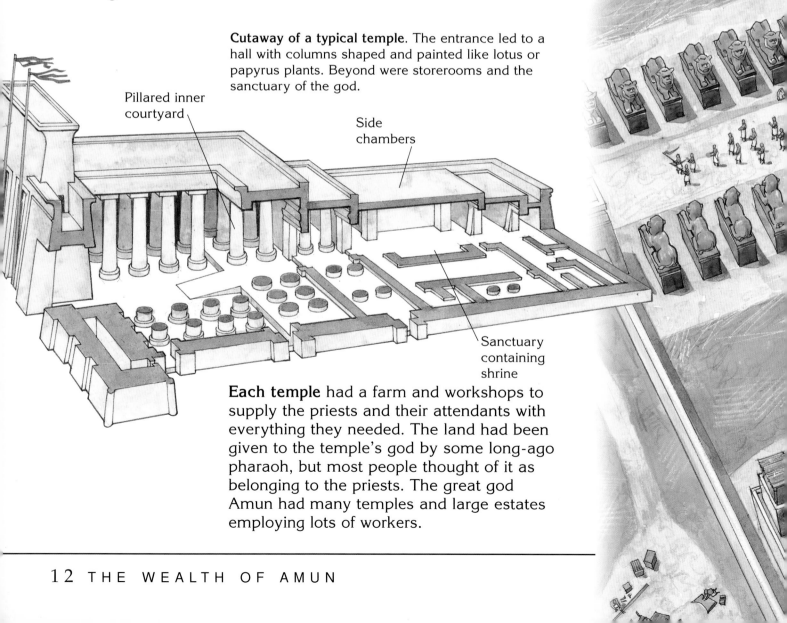

**Cutaway of a typical temple.** The entrance led to a hall with columns shaped and painted like lotus or papyrus plants. Beyond were storerooms and the sanctuary of the god.

Pillared inner courtyard

Side chambers

Sanctuary containing shrine

**Each temple** had a farm and workshops to supply the priests and their attendants with everything they needed. The land had been given to the temple's god by some long-ago pharaoh, but most people thought of it as belonging to the priests. The great god Amun had many temples and large estates employing lots of workers.

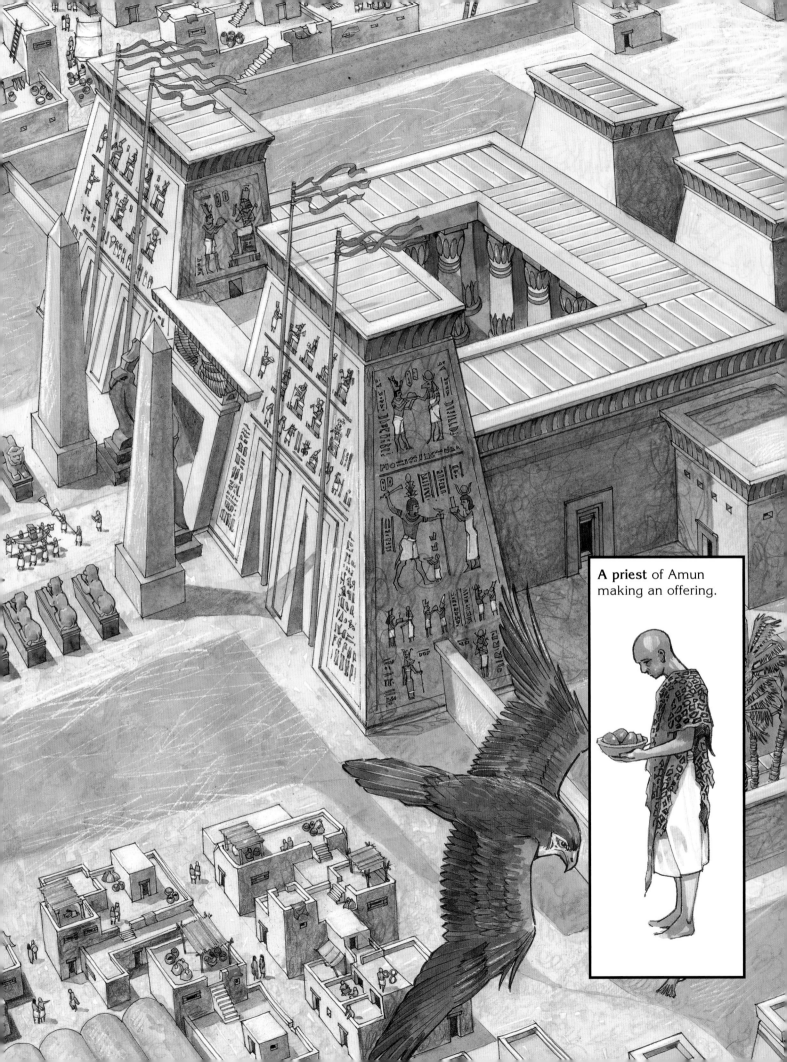

**A priest** of Amun making an offering.

# A NEW GOD

The ancient Egyptians had many gods and people believed it was right to honor them all. They were very troubled when a pharaoh called Akhnaten, who came to the throne in 1353 BCE, announced that their beliefs were wrong. He thought there was only one god, creator of everything, and since no other gods existed it was pointless to worship them. He identified this god with the Aten, which was the name of the disc of the sun. He shut Amun's temples and removed his name from all monuments. New temples were built for the Aten and a new capital city, called Akhtaten, was created in honor of the new god.

His people were confused and unhappy about this, but none were so hostile as the priests of Amun who lost their jobs and their very powerful position in Egyptian life.

Map of the excavated areas of Akhnaten's new city. Today its site is called Tell El-Amarna.

Left, wall relief shows Akhnaten and his queen, Nefertiti, receiving the gift of life from the hands of the Aten, through rays of its light.

Right, Nefertiti at the Great Temple of the Aten in the new city.

# THE BOY PHARAOH

Akhnaten was about thirty when he died in 1333 BCE, leaving a son of only about nine who became the new god-king. His name, Tutankhaten, meant "living image of the Aten." Little is known about his nine-year rule, but he must have faced many problems. Although still a child, he had to act as a wise, powerful ruler. Some of his ministers saw a chance to get more power by influencing him. His father, Akhnaten, preoccupied with religious reform, had governed badly. The army felt threatened by Egypt's enemies, the priests of the old gods were plotting to undo the reforms and ordinary people were hungry and unhappy. How could a boy rule all this? It seems that he didn't. Real control was taken by a relative called Ay, who may have been Queen Nefertiti's father, and the head of the army, General Horemheb.

Amenophis III
Queen Tye
Queen Nefertiti
Kiya, a minor wife of Akhnaten
Akhnaten
Tutankhamun
Smenkhare
Ankhesenamun

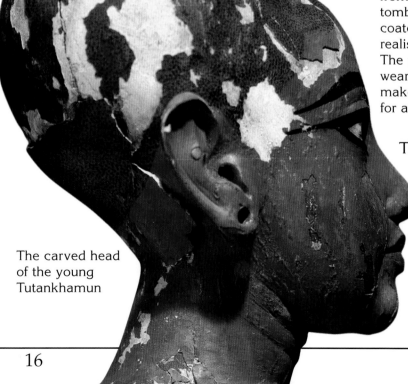

The carved head of the young Tutankhamun

16

**Left**, the face of Tutankhamun. It is a close-up of a portrait head, which was carved from wood, found in his tomb. The head is coated with gesso and realistically painted. The young pharaoh is wearing the heavy eye make-up that was usual for a wealthy Egyptian.

**Above**, Tutankhamun's family. Like most pharaohs, his father had several wives. Tutankhamun's mother was probably Kiya, a minor wife. Nefertiti only had daughters, one of whom married Tutankhamun.

The young pharaoh married his half-sister, Ankhesenamun, as pharaohs often did. Early in his reign came an important announcement: the pharaoh would not be called Tutankhaten any more. His name would be Tutankhamun or "living image of Amun." What he thought we will never know. But it showed that the Aten was no longer Egypt's only god. Amun's priests were regaining power.

# THE LIFE OF TUTANKHAMUN

**When** he was very young Tutankhamun was brought up with other Royal children in the women's quarters of the palace.

**He was** taught by tutors at the palace in a special school reserved for young princes and the sons of important nobles.

**Instructors** trained the young prince in archery and the use of weapons. He had to learn all the skills of a warrior.

**In 1335 BCE** his father died. Egyptian records show that for the next two years someone called Smenkhare was pharaoh.

**Smenkhare's** identity is a mystery. Was he a short-lived elder son of Akhnaten? Or did Queen Nefertiti, clinging to power, rule under that name?

**In 1333 BCE** Tutankhamun became pharaoh. In a ceremony at Thebes priests set the crowns of Egypt on the nine-year-old's head.

**At first** the new pharaoh was too young to be a real ruler. He carried out ceremonial duties and did as his advisors suggested.

**His queen,** Ankhesenamun, was one of the daughters of his father's chief wife, Nefertiti. They may have been married very young.

**Ankhesenamun** and Tutankhamun had two stillborn children. Their mummies were placed in their father's tomb.

**Tutankhamun's death**, in 1323 BCE, was mourned in the traditional way. Women wailed and threw ashes on their heads to show grief.

# A SUDDEN DEATH

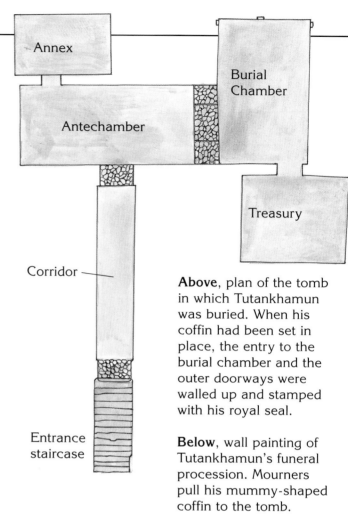

Tutankhamun was about eighteen when he died. He was buried hurriedly in a makeshift tomb. This was very odd. Normally great care was taken to prepare the royal burial place long before it was needed. Work on a tomb for Tutankhamun had only just begun when he died, so his death must have been unexpected. An existing tomb, intended for someone else and rather small, had to be adapted for him.

His death seems suspicious, especially as X-rays show a chip of bone inside his skull. Did he die from a blow to the head or was his skull damaged after his death? Did Ay, next in line to rule but already old, get tired of waiting for his turn? Did Amun's supporters or General Horemheb find the pharaoh less easy to influence as he grew up? These suspicions cannot be proved, but it is a fact that Ay and Horemheb became, in turn, Egypt's next pharaohs. All monuments to the Aten were destroyed and the names of Akhnaten and Tutankhamun were removed from every record, as though they had never existed.

**Above**, plan of the tomb in which Tutankhamun was buried. When his coffin had been set in place, the entry to the burial chamber and the outer doorways were walled up and stamped with his royal seal.

**Below**, wall painting of Tutankhamun's funeral procession. Mourners pull his mummy-shaped coffin to the tomb.

**Before burial** the Opening of the Mouth ceremony took place. A priest touched the mummy's face with ritual tools to restore its senses. A painting in the tomb shows Ay as the priest and Tutankhamun as Osiris, god of rebirth.

**Officials check** a list of items as Tutankhamun's "luggage" for the next world is put in place. It was a hard job fitting everything a pharaoh needed into such a small tomb. Six chariots were taken apart and stored in pieces.

# THE VALLEY OF THE KINGS

Centuries passed. There were strong pharaohs and weak ones. Egypt's glory faded, until, thirteen hundred years after Tutankhamun's death, it was swallowed up in the Roman Empire. Its history and customs were forgotten. Desert sand filled the valley where the pharaohs were buried and blotted out their tombs.

Only the great stone pyramids remained. From the 16th century, tales of its hidden wealth lured Europeans to Egypt in search of treasure. A few reached the Valley of the Kings, but the first person to link it with the pharaohs was a French Jesuit, Father Claude Sicard, who visited it in 1708 and described 10 open tombs.

By the early 20th century 61 of the valley's tombs had been uncovered. By then the diggers were not gold-seekers but archaeologists who preserved and studied everything they found. Yet in a sense they were treasure hunters too. All the tombs they found had already been robbed of their contents. It was every archaeologist's dream to find one that hadn't. By 1922 it seemed as if all the valley had been excavated, but Howard Carter, an English archaeologist, was not going to give up hope.

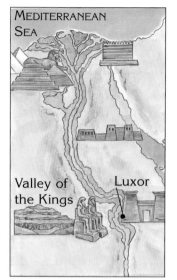

MEDITERRANEAN SEA

Valley of the Kings

Luxor

Left, map showing the Valley of the Kings, near the modern city of Luxor. Local interest in the tombs really started when foreigners began digging there, and in the 19th century thousands of ancient pieces, and even whole mummies, were sold to them. This is now banned.

Below, the valley with some of the tombs found there from 1900 to 1922.

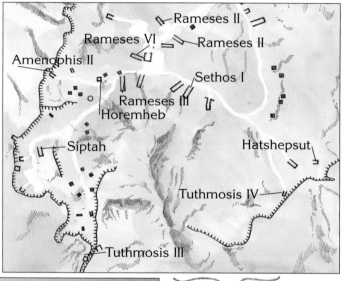

Rameses II
Rameses VI
Rameses II
Amenophis II
Sethos I
Rameses III
Horemheb
Siptah
Hatshepsut
Tuthmosis IV
Tuthmosis III

**Above**, this little cup, found in the valley in 1906, bears the name of Tutankhamun. It was the first clue that his tomb was nearby. Right, the valley as it is today.

Collar of flowers

Linen bags containing natron

Pottery vessels

**More clues** to Tutankhamun: objects found in 1907 that had been buried in a pit. One bore his name.

# THE LIFE OF HOWARD CARTER

**Howard Carter** was born in London in 1874. His father was a painter and illustrator.

**Carter** grew up in a Norfolk village. He had no formal education and always regretted this.

**He was 17** when the Egyptologist Percy Newbury spotted his drawing skills.

**Newbury employed** Carter to ink in tracings of tomb scenes brought back from Egypt.

**Carter** was still only 17 when he arrived in Egypt to draw and help in excavations.

**Carter** was so keen on archaeology that he spent the next six years copying scenes.

**In 1899** Carter became Inspector of Monuments for the Egyptian Antiquities Service.

**His work** in the Valley of the Kings included the safe removal of some royal mummies.

**In 1905** he got into trouble for expelling rowdy tourists from a tomb and resigned.

**Very hard up** as a result, he had the luck to be introduced to Lord Carnarvon.

**Carnarvon** took up excavating to pass the time. Soon he had got together a large team.

**As well** as Carter, the expert, Carnarvon's wife, servants, doctor and cook came along.

Lord Carnarvon, a rich English aristocrat, had gone to Egypt for his health and enjoyed doing some excavating. He hired Carter to find likely sites for him. Working together from 1907 they made many finds but not the one they wanted – the tomb of the unknown pharaoh whose name was on objects found in the valley. By 1922 Carnarvon was ready to give up. The hunt was too expensive. But Carter persuaded him to have one last try.

**1922:** Carter shows where he plans to make the last dig and offers to pay for it himself.

**Carnarvon relents** and pays. Soon, to his joy, Carter uncovers a door stamped with this seal.

# UNSEALING THE TOMB

It was 4 November 1922 when Carter and his team, digging with failing hopes, uncovered the top of a staircase. Sixteen steps led down to a sealed door. Carter immediately sent a telegram to Carnarvon in England: "At last have made wonderful discovery ...a magnificent tomb with seals intact." Then he spent 20 days in agonizing suspense, waiting for Carnarvon to join him. Both of them had to be there for the great moment—the opening of the tomb.

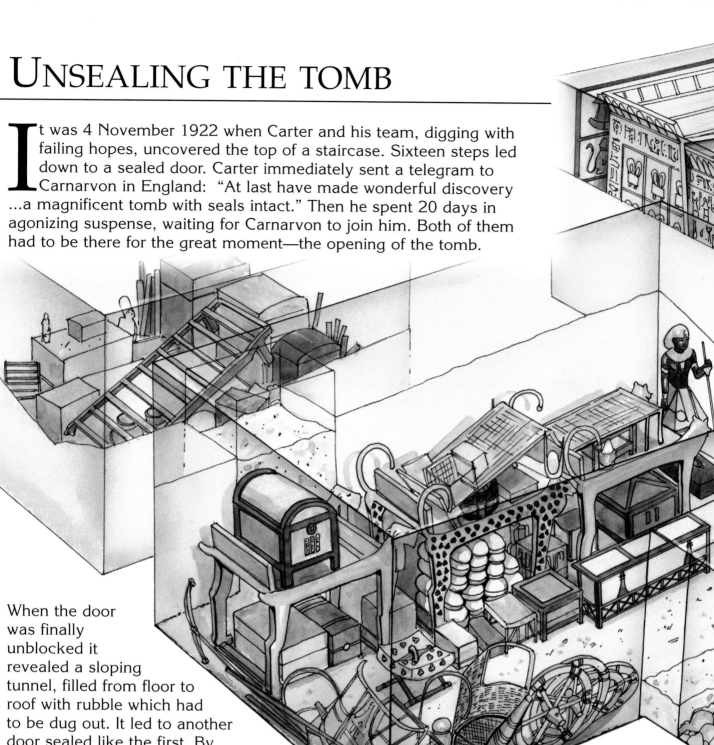

When the door was finally unblocked it revealed a sloping tunnel, filled from floor to roof with rubble which had to be dug out. It led to another door sealed like the first. By November 26th, the tunnel was clear and Carter and Carnarvon started to unblock the second door. Carter prised out a few stones, put a candle through the hole he had made and peered into the dark. At first the flame flickered so much he could not see clearly. When he did, he could not speak for amazement. Unable to stand the suspense Carnarvon asked "Can you see anything?" Carter's breathless reply has become famous: "Yes, wonderful things."

**Before** the doors were opened Carter knew he had found the tomb he had been seeking for so long, for the seals on the doors bore the name of Tutankhamun. But he also realized the tomb had been broken into in ancient times, because both doors had been patched and resealed with a later seal. This was only to be expected. An untouched tomb was too much to hope for. But when he peered into the darkness and saw statues, strange animal shapes, and "everywhere a glint of gold," he knew his dream had come true.

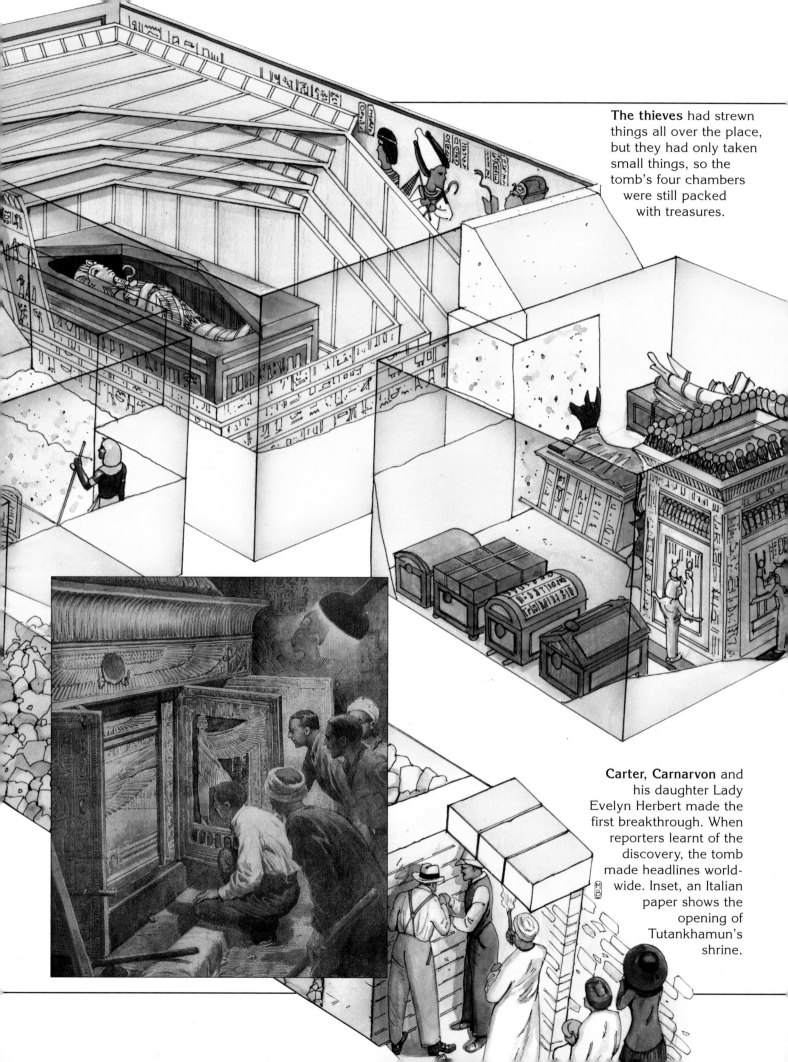

**The thieves** had strewn things all over the place, but they had only taken small things, so the tomb's four chambers were still packed with treasures.

**Carter, Carnarvon** and his daughter Lady Evelyn Herbert made the first breakthrough. When reporters learnt of the discovery, the tomb made headlines world-wide. Inset, an Italian paper shows the opening of Tutankhamun's shrine.

# STEPPING INSIDE

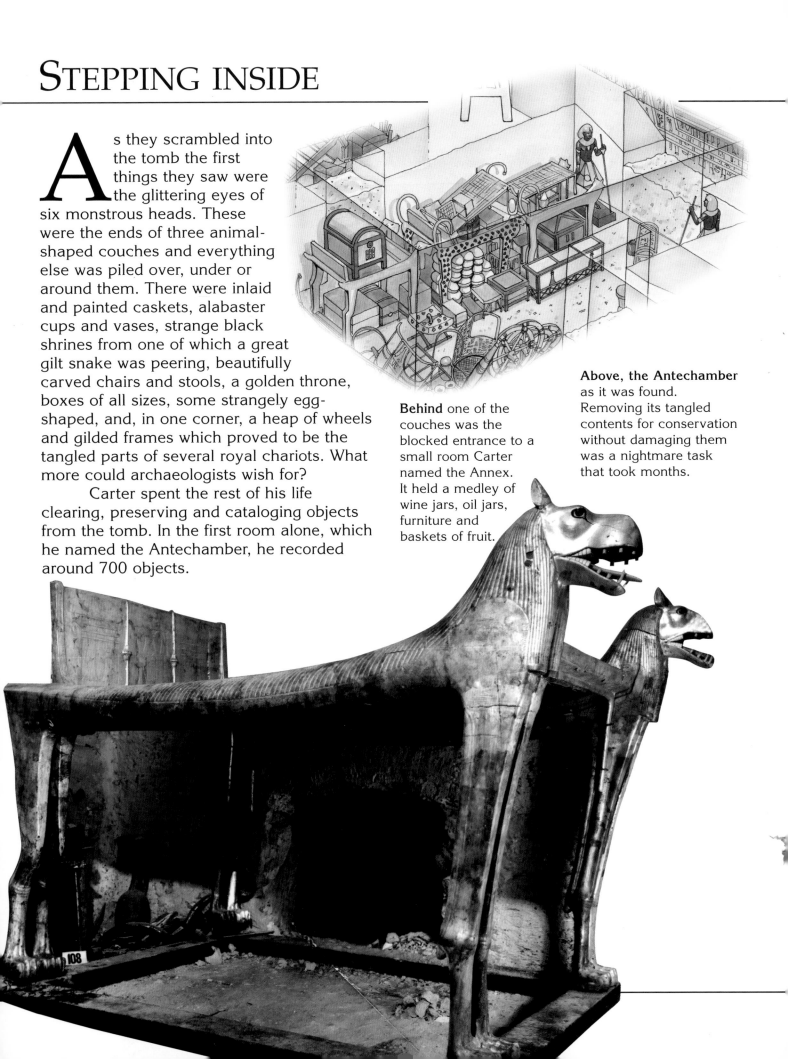

As they scrambled into the tomb the first things they saw were the glittering eyes of six monstrous heads. These were the ends of three animal-shaped couches and everything else was piled over, under or around them. There were inlaid and painted caskets, alabaster cups and vases, strange black shrines from one of which a great gilt snake was peering, beautifully carved chairs and stools, a golden throne, boxes of all sizes, some strangely egg-shaped, and, in one corner, a heap of wheels and gilded frames which proved to be the tangled parts of several royal chariots. What more could archaeologists wish for?

Carter spent the rest of his life clearing, preserving and cataloging objects from the tomb. In the first room alone, which he named the Antechamber, he recorded around 700 objects.

**Behind** one of the couches was the blocked entrance to a small room Carter named the Annex. It held a medley of wine jars, oil jars, furniture and baskets of fruit.

**Above, the Antechamber** as it was found. Removing its tangled contents for conservation without damaging them was a nightmare task that took months.

**Reconstructed** chariot. The gilded body is inlaid with colored glass and carnelian.

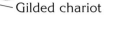
Gilded chariot

**Below, there were** many kinds of weapon in the tomb, some for warfare, some, such as throw-sticks, for hunting, some for royal ceremonies:
a) sword;
b) and c) spear heads;
d) ceremonial dagger;
e) club with hand guard;
f) battle axe;
g) club with projecting blade.

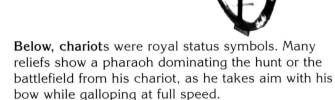

**Below, chariot**s were royal status symbols. Many reliefs show a pharaoh dominating the hunt or the battlefield from his chariot, as he takes aim with his bow while galloping at full speed.

**Left**, box of writing tools: pencase (for rush pens), palettes (holding cakes of ink) and papyrus smoother.

These treasures were wonderful, but there was much more in store. On the end wall of the Antechamber two life-size, black and gold figures of the pharaoh guarded a walled-up entrance. This, Carter felt sure, was the door of the burial chamber.

**The pharaoh** used ointments and eye make-up. This stand holds jars of scented oil.

**Left**, small shrines held ritual figures like this gilded image of the pharaoh, draped in a linen shawl.

**Above**, an ivory-veneered game box.

**Left**, food for the spirit: fruit, bread, meat, beans and lentils, spices and honey.

# THE BURIAL CHAMBER

After clearing the entrance to the Burial Chamber Carter and his team saw what seemed like a wall of gold. In fact it was one side of a gilded shrine that almost filled the room. The shrine's double doors were bolted but the stamped cord which should have sealed them was gone. The thieves had broken in here too. But Carter's dismay did not last long – inside that first shrine was a second with the seal intact. So the thieves had not robbed it. This shrine was covered by a wooden framework over which was a pall of dark linen spangled with bronze sequins. In the second shrine was a third and inside that was a fourth. All were of carved and gilded wooden panels, decorated inside and out with sacred texts, symbols and figures of Tutankhamun with gods and goddesses. The inner shrine covered a sarcophagus carved from a block of quartzite so huge the shrine barely fitted round it. When the sarcophagus lid was eventually lifted, the most amazing sight of all was revealed – three magnificent coffins, one inside the other, protecting the mummified body of the young pharaoh.

**The outer**, cedar wood shrine was carved with protective amulets to form a gilded openwork pattern on a blue faience ground.

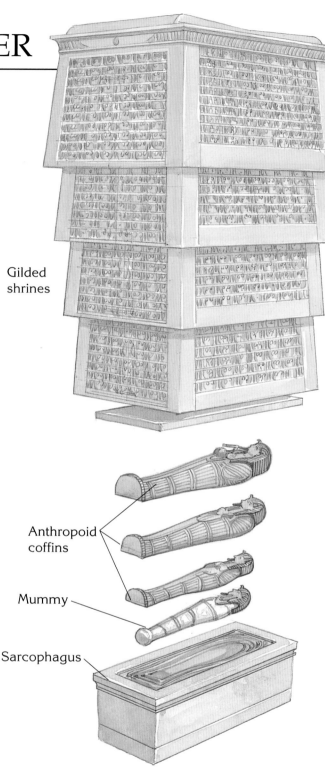

Gilded shrines

Anthropoid coffins

Mummy

Sarcophagus

**Above**, the shrines within shrines which enclosed the quartzite sarcophagus in which were coffins within coffins. The shrines had been taken into the chamber in sections and assembled there. Removing the panels for conservation was difficult. "We had to squeeze in and out like weasels" said Carter, "and work in all kinds of embarrassing positions."

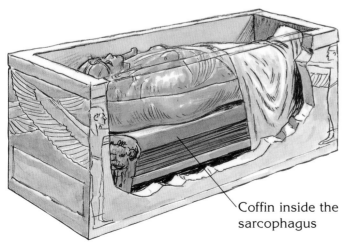

Coffin inside the sarcophagus

**The pharaoh's** golden-yellow sarcophagus is embraced by the outstretched wings of four goddesses carved in high relief who stand at its corners. They are Isis, Nepthys, Selkis and Neith, who, according to ancient Egyptian myth, watched over the dead.

**The sarcophagus's** red granite lid looked as if it had originally come from another one and had been painted to match. It had split as it was being put in place, probably because the toe of the outer coffin stuck up too far The toe was chopped level, the lid replaced and the crack covered with tinted plaster.

# THE LAYERED COFFINS

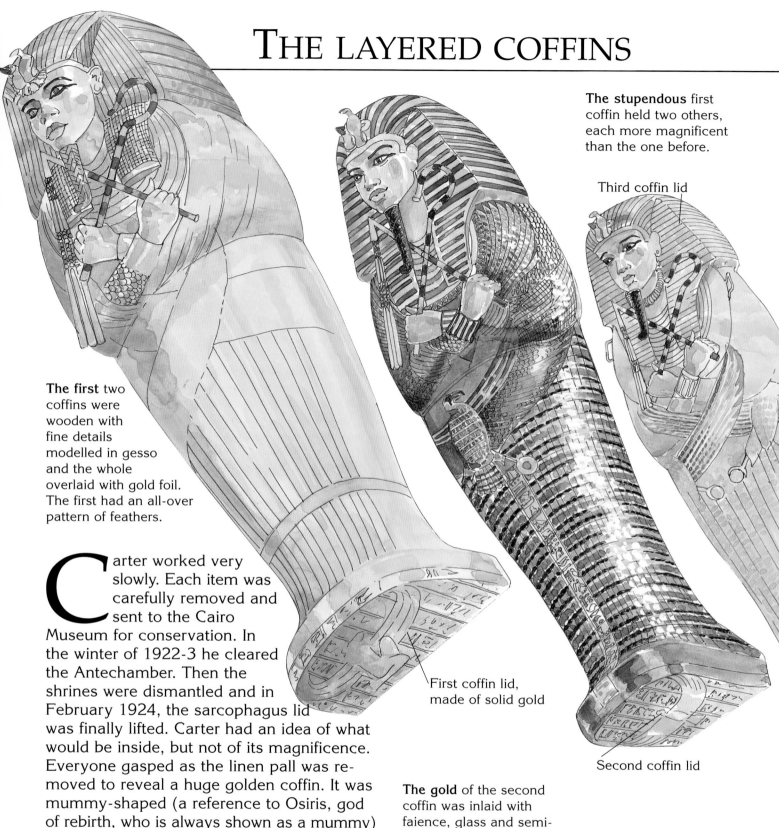

**The stupendous** first coffin held two others, each more magnificent than the one before.

Third coffin lid

**The first** two coffins were wooden with fine details modelled in gesso and the whole overlaid with gold foil. The first had an all-over pattern of feathers.

First coffin lid, made of solid gold

Second coffin lid

Carter worked very slowly. Each item was carefully removed and sent to the Cairo Museum for conservation. In the winter of 1922-3 he cleared the Antechamber. Then the shrines were dismantled and in February 1924, the sarcophagus lid was finally lifted. Carter had an idea of what would be inside, but not of its magnificence. Everyone gasped as the linen pall was removed to reveal a huge golden coffin. It was mummy-shaped (a reference to Osiris, god of rebirth, who is always shown as a mummy) with the face of Tutankhamun. His crossed hands held the royal crook and flail, and on his forehead his kingdom's emblems—the cobra of Lower Egypt and the vulture of Upper Egypt—were garlanded with olive leaves and cornflowers.

**The gold** of the second coffin was inlaid with faience, glass and semi-precious stones. The mask's broad collar and bracelets and every feather of the pattern was picked out in jasper-red, lapis-blue and turquoise glass.

**Lifting** the last pall revealed an astonishing surprise – the innermost coffin was made of solid gold, so heavy that eight men could barely lift it.

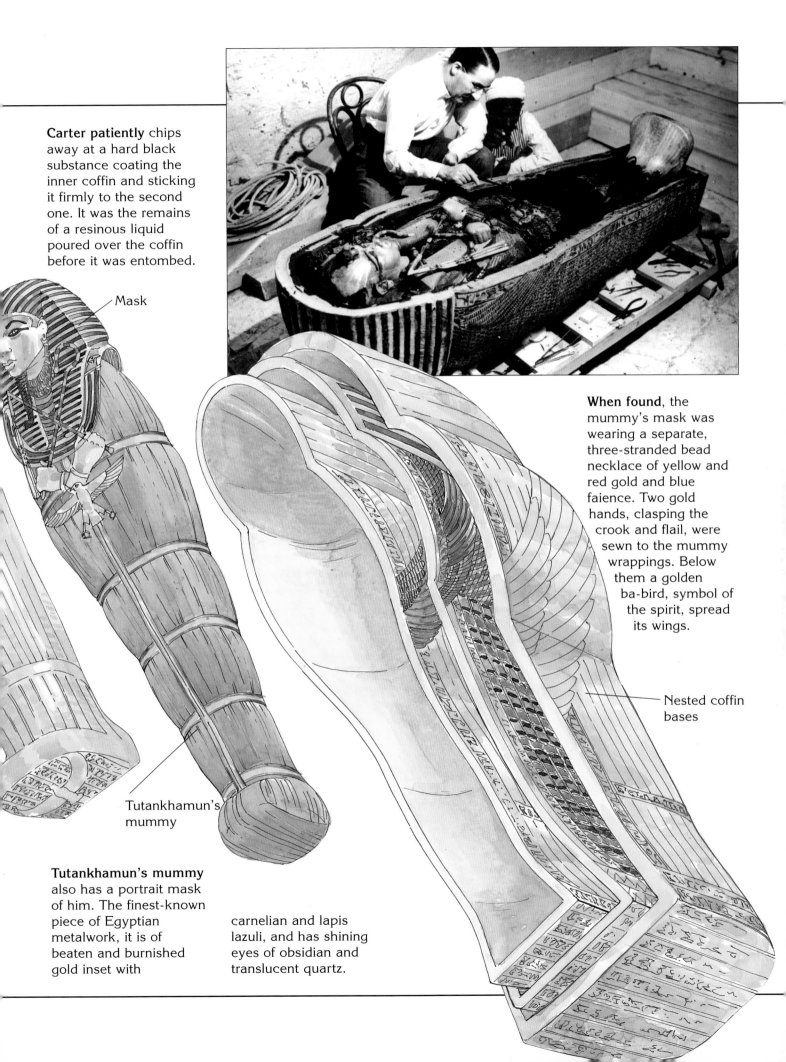

**Carter patiently** chips away at a hard black substance coating the inner coffin and sticking it firmly to the second one. It was the remains of a resinous liquid poured over the coffin before it was entombed.

Mask

Tutankhamun's mummy

**Tutankhamun's mummy** also has a portrait mask of him. The finest-known piece of Egyptian metalwork, it is of beaten and burnished gold inset with carnelian and lapis lazuli, and has shining eyes of obsidian and translucent quartz.

**When found**, the mummy's mask was wearing a separate, three-stranded bead necklace of yellow and red gold and blue faience. Two gold hands, clasping the crook and flail, were sewn to the mummy wrappings. Below them a golden ba-bird, symbol of the spirit, spread its wings.

Nested coffin bases

# THE MUMMY

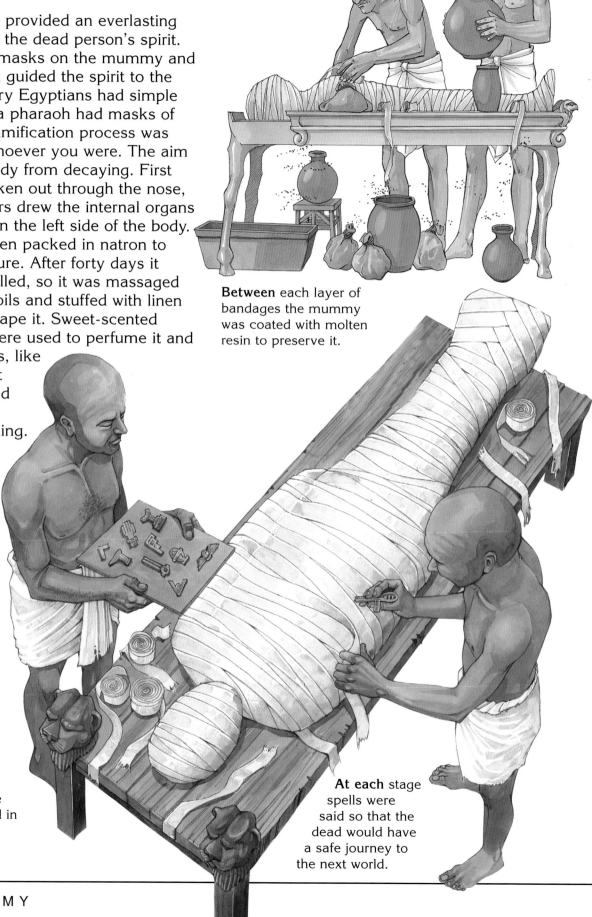

A mummy provided an everlasting body for the dead person's spirit. Portrait masks on the mummy and its coffin guided the spirit to the right body. Ordinary Egyptians had simple painted portraits, a pharaoh had masks of gold, but the mummification process was much the same whoever you were. The aim was to stop the body from decaying. First the brains were taken out through the nose, then the embalmers drew the internal organs out through a slit in the left side of the body. The corpse was then packed in natron to draw out its moisture. After forty days it was dry but shrivelled, so it was massaged with preservative oils and stuffed with linen or sawdust to reshape it. Sweet-scented spices and wine were used to perfume it and any missing pieces, like fingers or toes that sometimes dropped off, were replaced with wood or padding. Now very lifelike, the body was tightly wrapped in yards of linen bandages.

**Between** each layer of bandages the mummy was coated with molten resin to preserve it.

**Wrapping** the mummy took up to fifteen days. Everything had to be done according to ancient rules.

**Amulets** (magic charms) of various shapes, each with its own special protective powers, were wrapped in among the bandages.

**At each** stage spells were said so that the dead would have a safe journey to the next world.

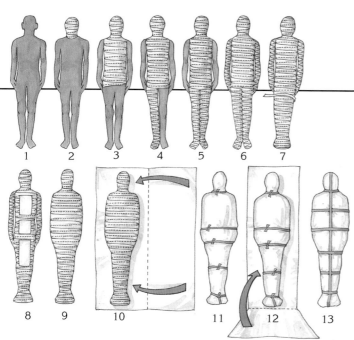

**The gold mask** faithfully portrays Tutankhamun's features, since the face is the same on the first and third coffins. The face on the middle coffin is different, which suggests it was made for another pharaoh.

**Wrapping a mummy:** The embalmed body (1) had its head wrapped (2), then its torso (3). Its legs were wrapped separately (4 & 5), then its arms (6) and then both legs together (7).

Pads were added and the mummy rewrapped (8 & 9), then covered in a shroud (10), and tied (11). A second shroud (12) was secured with bands (13).

Mummification re-enacted the fate of Osiris, king of the dead and lord of rebirth. He was murdered and cut into pieces by his jealous brother Set. After Anubis, the jackal-headed god, bound the pieces together, his sister Isis restored him to life. After the embalmers finished their work, a priest in a jackal mask played the role of Anubis and performed ceremonial rites and said prayers over the mummy.

**Photograph** of Tutankhamun's skull taken when his mummy was unwrapped in 1925. The nose has been flattened by the pressure of the linen wrappings. An X-ray taken in 1968 showed a fragment of bone inside the skull (see p.18). Did the embalmers cause it, was it due to a fatal accident, or a blow meant to kill him? No one will ever know.

# THE AMULETS

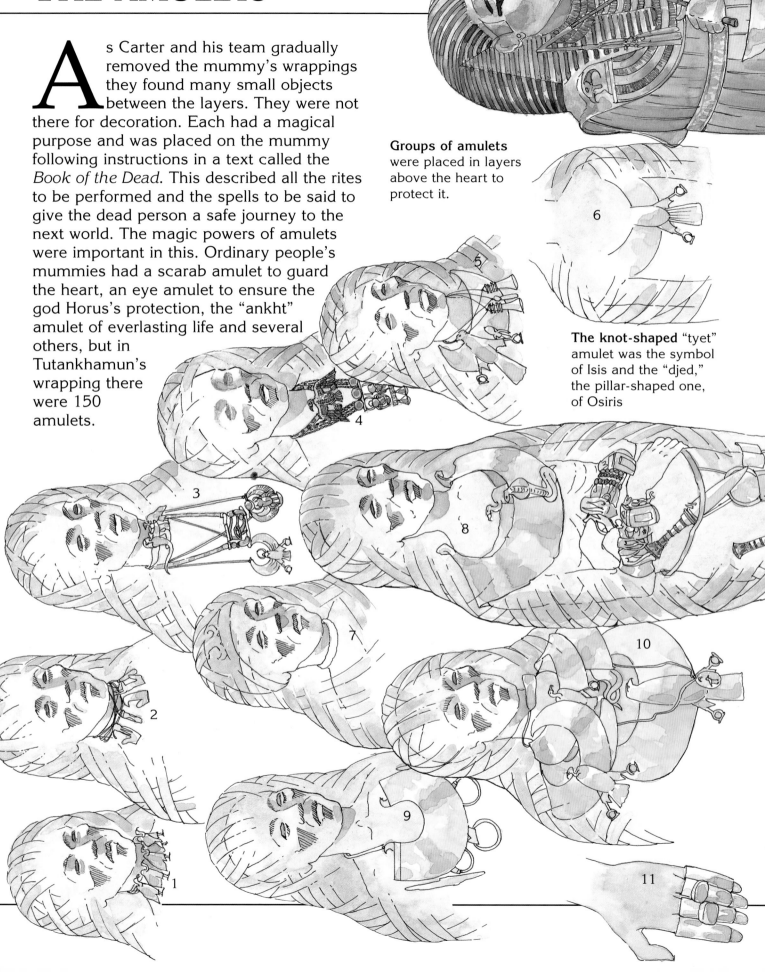

As Carter and his team gradually removed the mummy's wrappings they found many small objects between the layers. They were not there for decoration. Each had a magical purpose and was placed on the mummy following instructions in a text called the *Book of the Dead*. This described all the rites to be performed and the spells to be said to give the dead person a safe journey to the next world. The magic powers of amulets were important in this. Ordinary people's mummies had a scarab amulet to guard the heart, an eye amulet to ensure the god Horus's protection, the "ankht" amulet of everlasting life and several others, but in Tutankhamun's wrapping there were 150 amulets.

**Groups of amulets** were placed in layers above the heart to protect it.

**The knot-shaped** "tyet" amulet was the symbol of Isis and the "djed," the pillar-shaped one, of Osiris

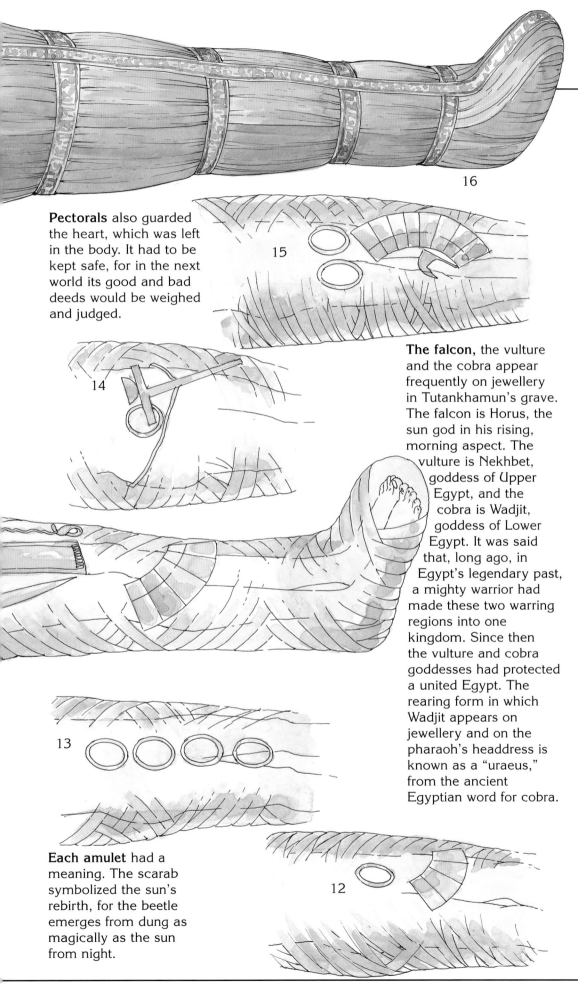

**Pectorals** also guarded the heart, which was left in the body. It had to be kept safe, for in the next world its good and bad deeds would be weighed and judged.

**The falcon,** the vulture and the cobra appear frequently on jewellery in Tutankhamun's grave. The falcon is Horus, the sun god in his rising, morning aspect. The vulture is Nekhbet, goddess of Upper Egypt, and the cobra is Wadjit, goddess of Lower Egypt. It was said that, long ago, in Egypt's legendary past, a mighty warrior had made these two warring regions into one kingdom. Since then the vulture and cobra goddesses had protected a united Egypt. The rearing form in which Wadjit appears on jewellery and on the pharaoh's headdress is known as a "uraeus," from the ancient Egyptian word for cobra.

**Each amulet** had a meaning. The scarab symbolized the sun's rebirth, for the beetle emerges from dung as magically as the sun from night.

Key
1 four vulture amulets, one uraeus amulet
2 Thoth amulet, serpent-head amulet, falcon-head amulet, Anubis amulet, wadj-scepter amulet
3 wedjat-eye pectoral, scarab pectoral, falcon pectoral, human-headed winged uraeus amulet, double uraeus amulet, vulture amulet
4 vulture pectoral, scarab pectoral
5 vulture collar, wadj-sceptre amulet, djed-pillar amulet, tyet-knot amulet
6 falcon collar
7 bead-work cap
8 uraeus collar, vulture collar, eight bracelets, girdle, two daggers, apron, bracelet, two falcon collars
9 falcon collar, bracelets with lapis-lazuli and carnelian beads
10 amuletic knots
11 sheet-gold finger stalls, heavy signet rings
12 falcon collar, circlet
13 four circlets
14 faience broad collar, T-shaped amulet, circlet, girdle
15 two falcon collars, two circlets
16 mummy case of Tutankhamun with death mask inlaid with sheet gold

# MEETING THE GODS

The walls of the Burial Chamber show the results of the pharaoh's funeral rites. His body has been preserved, so his spirit has recognized and returned to it; the perils of the journey to the next world have been overcome thanks to all the amulets; his heart has been weighed in the scales of truth and is good. So now the gods will receive him. One wall shows mourners taking him to the tomb (the scene on p.18). The two long walls show the gods welcoming him. The fourth wall shows the pharaoh's final glory: he will share the sun's boat as it passes under the world by night, along the river that flows through the Land of the Dead and appears again at dawn. The paintings' purpose was magical: by showing what should happen they ensured that it did. Once the tomb was sealed no one would see them, but that did not matter, for they would be serving the purpose they were created for.

**Above**, plastering the tomb's walls.

**Left**, mixing colors.

**Below**, the sun (as a scarab) begins its journey through the night, a journey of rebirth which the pharaoh will share. The baboons are the twelve gods of the first hour of the night.

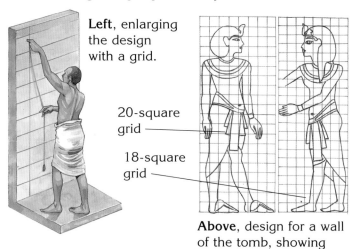

**Left**, enlarging the design with a grid.

20-square grid

18-square grid

**Above**, design for a wall of the tomb, showing the 20-square grid of the Akhnaten period and the more traditional 18-square grid used in Tutankhamun's tomb.

Draughtsmen copied the designs onto the wall by means of a grid. Painters filled in the outline with colors made from ground minerals mixed with gum or egg white. Similar scenes are found in many tombs, changing little over the centuries. Artists followed strict guidelines. If the images were incorrect the magic would not work.

**The Chamber** as it is today. A reinforced glass lid shields the outer coffin in the sarcophagus.

**In the center** of the long wall behind it, Nut, the goddess of the night, is welcoming Tutankhamun.

**To the left**, the pharaoh, accompanied by his "ka" (his spirit double), is embracing the god Osiris.

**To the right**, the pharaoh's "Osiris" mummy receives the Opening of the Mouth from Ay (not shown).

**On the opposite** wall Tutankhamun is welcomed to the underworld by Hathor, chief goddess of the Land of the Dead. The jackal-headed figure behind her is the embalmer god, Anubis. On the left Isis waits to greet the dead pharaoh. Behind her sit three minor gods. The painting was damaged when the wall was dismantled to allow the shrines to be taken out.

# A GILDED SHRINE

**A** small room (Carter called it the Treasury) led off the burial chamber. Just inside, gazing at all who entered, lay a jackal on a shrine. This was Anubis, god of the the dead. Beside him stood magnificent wood and ivory caskets and many coffin-shaped boxes and small black shrines, some with model boats on them. Then Carter saw "the most beautiful monument I have ever seen."

Shrine

**A canopy** of four posts supporting a cornice with a frieze of rearing cobras covered the shrine, which stood on a sled. Between the posts the four guardian goddesses stretched out their arms protectively.

What Carter saw was the shrine to hold the pharaoh's internal organs. The organs were removed during mummification, preserved and placed in the tomb, so the body would be complete in the afterlife. The liver, lungs stomach and intestines were dried, wrapped and stored in four containers, called canopic jars. In ordinary funerals the jars were put in the tomb in a box, but a pharaoh needed something grander. Under a magnificent canopy, the gilded canopic shrine held a hollow chest carved from a block of semi-translucent quartzite. It was inscribed with sacred texts and at each corner the guardian goddesses, Isis, Nepthys, Selkis and Neith, embraced it with open arms (below).

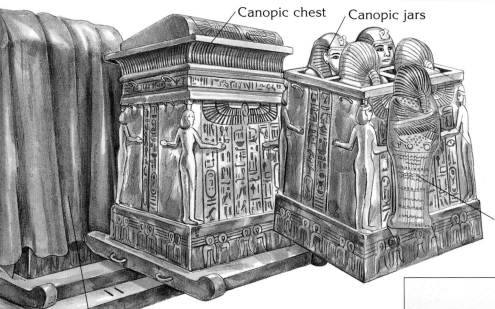

Canopic chest     Canopic jars

Linen cloth

a            b       c

**One** of the tiny coffins.
a) outside of base and lid
b) inside of base and lid
c) the mummified organ

Diagram showing how the canopic jars were inserted

**The gilded walls** of the shrine were decorated in sunken relief with figures of the four goddesses and the four protector spirits of the canopic jars. Inside the shrine a linen cloth covered the chest.

**Beneath** the lid of the chest were four human-headed stoppers closing four compartments hollowed in the block. Each hollow held a tiny coffin of beaten gold.

**One** of the 18 boats found in the Treasury. It symbolizes both the voyage to the next world and the boat of the sun.

# TOMB ROBBERS

From the resealed doorway Carter and Carnarvon knew thieves had been into the tomb. The design on the seals told Carter the break-in was soon after Tutankhamun's death. The officials who resealed the tomb had had its entrance passage filled with rubble as an extra safeguard. Their scheme did not work, for soon afterwards a second gang tunnelled in through the rubble. Ancient Egyptian records of robberies show they were sometimes committed by the craftsmen who built the tombs, so perhaps Tutankhamun was robbed by the people who helped to bury him. The robbers wanted small objects – jewellery, fine linen (very valuable), cosmetic oils, glass (rare) and gold. They were probably working fast for fear of the valley's police, for if tomb robbers had time they hacked shrines and coffins to pieces and burnt them to get the melted gold.

**The worst confusion** was in the Annex, which had been overfilled in a disorganized way at the outset. Although intended as a food store, lots of other things had been crammed in too. The thieves turned all this upside down.

**This photo** of the Antechamber as Carter found it shows the sort of hasty tidying the Valley Police did after the second burglary. The Annex was in an even worse state. The thieves had trampled over everything to get what they wanted. Furniture, oil and wine jars, baskets of fruit and bread, stools, chairs and bedsteads and boxes of assorted objects were left in a hopeless tangle. The thieves went through everything, tipping the contents out of boxes, breaking things, flinging aside what they did not want and leaving objects piled up chaotically.

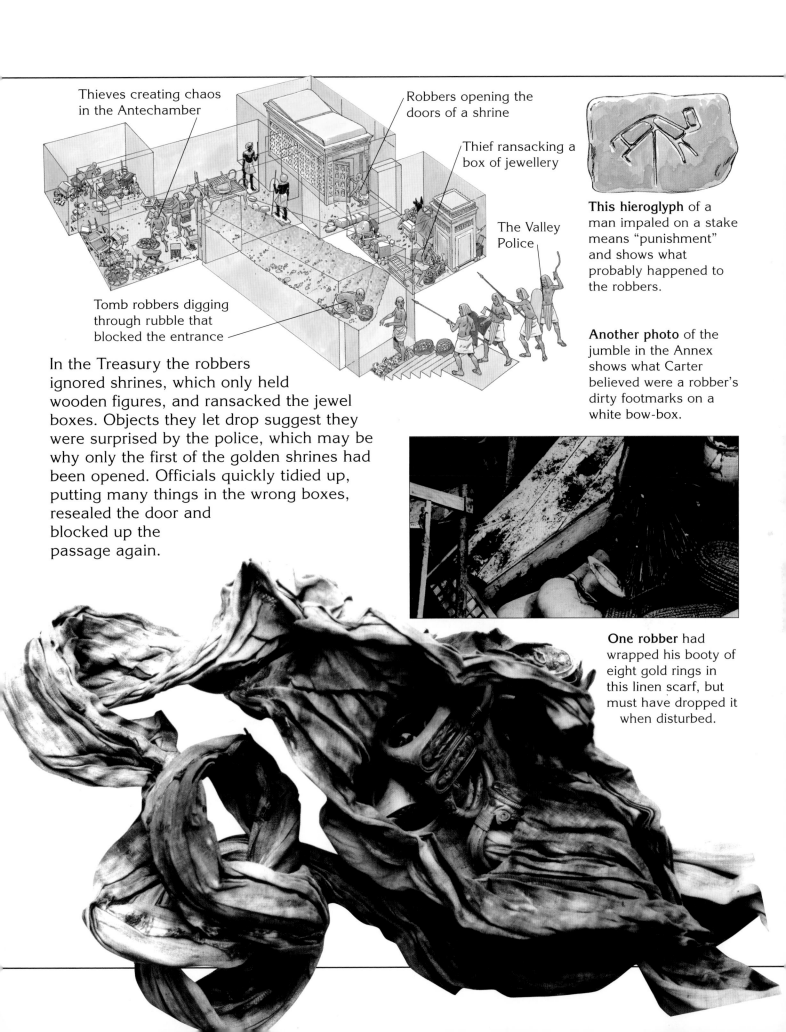

Thieves creating chaos in the Antechamber

Robbers opening the doors of a shrine

Thief ransacking a box of jewellery

The Valley Police

Tomb robbers digging through rubble that blocked the entrance

**This hieroglyph** of a man impaled on a stake means "punishment" and shows what probably happened to the robbers.

**Another photo** of the jumble in the Annex shows what Carter believed were a robber's dirty footmarks on a white bow-box.

In the Treasury the robbers ignored shrines, which only held wooden figures, and ransacked the jewel boxes. Objects they let drop suggest they were surprised by the police, which may be why only the first of the golden shrines had been opened. Officials quickly tidied up, putting many things in the wrong boxes, resealed the door and blocked up the passage again.

**One robber** had wrapped his booty of eight gold rings in this linen scarf, but must have dropped it when disturbed.

# TREASURES OF THE TOMB

The contents of Tutankhamun's tomb outshone all previous Egyptian finds. Yet they were the robbers' leftovers. From some original dockets Carter estimated that 60% of the jewellery had gone. Even so, over 200 superb pieces remained, as well as the pieces in the mummy wrappings. Carter summed up the amazement (and regret) that the tomb's contents still inspire: "If they could bury this unimportant king with so much splendor, whatever must the tomb of a well-established pharaoh have looked like?"

Lucky accidents saved the treasures. If the robbers had not been caught they would have taken more. If Tutankhamun's father had not made hated reforms, his son's burial place would not have been forgotten. If it had been known, a new tomb would not have been cut just above it, burying its entrance. If there had been a hint of an entrance, later robbers would have stolen everything. If anyone less painstaking than Carter had excavated it, the contents might have been seriously damaged. Now, marvellously preserved in the Cairo Museum, they are one of the wonders of the world.

**Right**, this is the back panel of a sumptuously inlaid armchair known as the Golden Throne, described by Lord Carnarvon as "one of the most marvellous pieces of furniture that has ever been discovered." It is made of wood overlaid with sheet gold and silver which is inset with colored glass, faience and semi-precious stones. Lion heads flank the seat and its winged arms bear the double crown of Lower and Upper Egypt. The scene on the back shows Tutankhamun and Ankhesenamun his queen in an open-air pavilion. Unlike the rigid pharaoh-images of most ancient Egyptian art, the king is shown comfortably seated while his wife rubs perfumed oil over him. Above them the Aten pours down its life-giving rays.

**Detail of a gold** pectoral from the Treasury that one of the thieves left behind. A large piece of lapis lazuli forms the scarab. Its wings are of inlaid gold, set with carnelian, turquoise and lapis lazuli.

# EGYPTOMANIA

As photos of the fabulous objects appeared in the press, the craze of "Egyptomania" swept Europe and America. People danced the "Tutankhamun rag," cinemas were designed like Egyptian temples, clothes, jewellery, fabrics and decoration all got the Egyptian touch. The story had everything: a forgotten boy-king, unbelievable treasures, and now a "mummy's curse." In 1923 Lord Carnarvon, already an invalid, died of pneumonia, following a blood infection caused by a mosquito bite. Was this the pharaoh's vengeance? People remembered many "omens." It was said that a cobra ate Carnarvon's pet canary on the day of the discovery. After that the death of anyone connected with the discovery was seen as proof of the curse – and with so many people involved some were bound to die. Carter, however, lived till 1939 after dedicating the rest of his life to studying the tomb. The treasures have been removed, but Tutankhamun, their one-time owner, still rests in his coffin in the Valley of the Kings.

**Above**, Lord Carnarvon resting on the veranda of Carter's house. Badly hurt in a car accident in 1901, he had been in poor health ever since.

TUTANKHAMUN IN FASHION

**1923** American fashions include frocks with "vari-colored Luxor motifs."

**Wrap-over** coat with "the decorative splendor of the Tutankhamun" era.

**Beading**, bobbed hair and droopy skirts all had Egyptian inspiration.

**1924** Elegant women had tired of Tut. He was no longer fashionable.

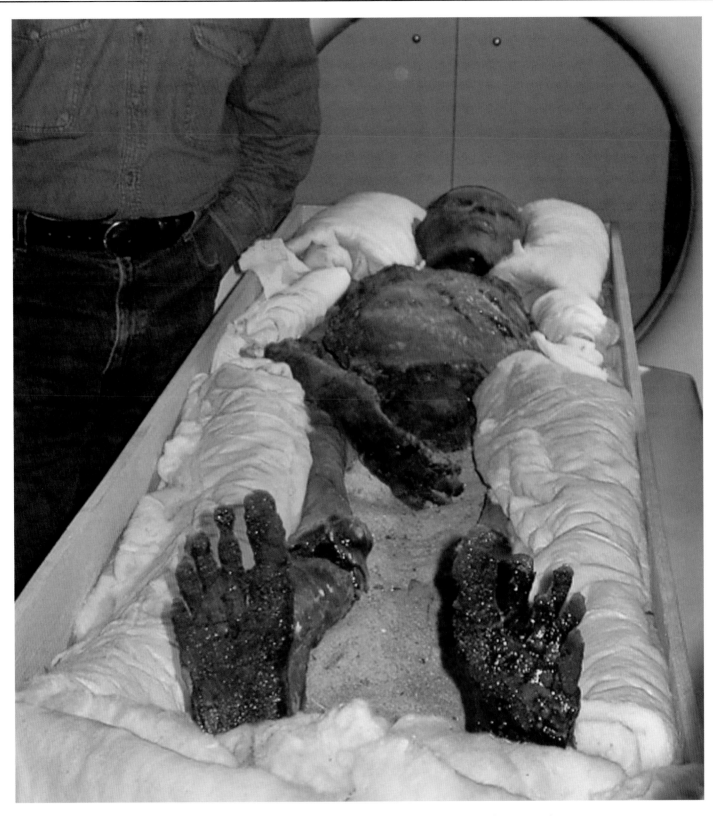

Tutankhamun's life and the mysteries surrounding his death have fascinated
people all over the world since the discovery of his tomb in 1922. In January 2005,
Egyptian researchers conducted a CT scan of the 3,300 year-old mummy, which
could provide answers to the questions surrounding Tutankhamun's life and death.

# THE STORY OF THE TOMB

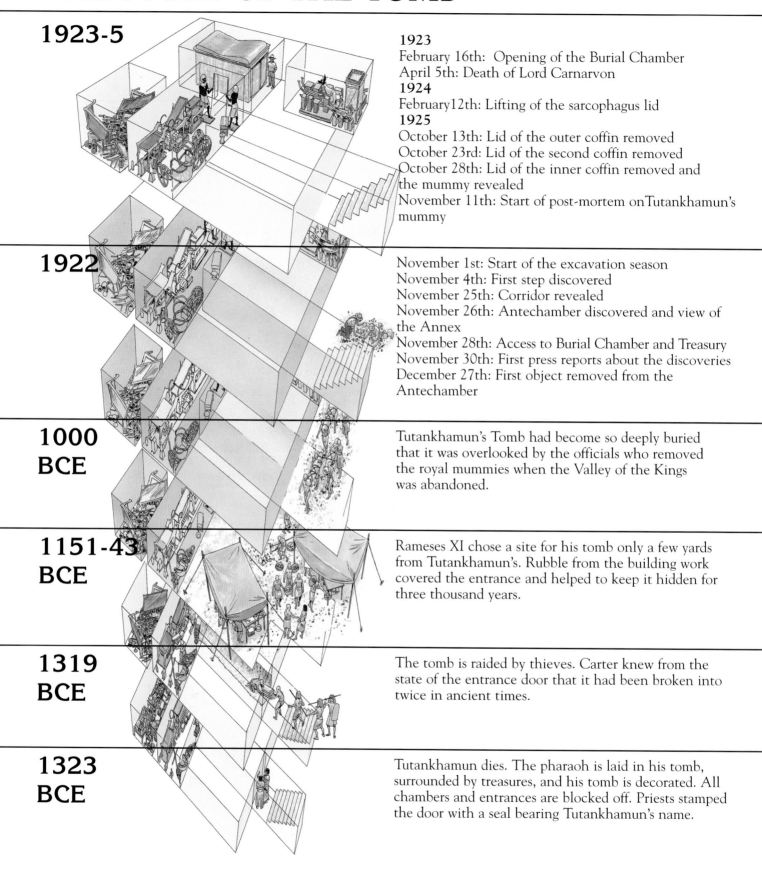

**1923-5**

1923
February 16th:  Opening of the Burial Chamber
April 5th: Death of Lord Carnarvon
**1924**
February 12th: Lifting of the sarcophagus lid
**1925**
October 13th: Lid of the outer coffin removed
October 23rd: Lid of the second coffin removed
October 28th: Lid of the inner coffin removed and
the mummy revealed
November 11th: Start of post-mortem on Tutankhamun's
mummy

**1922**

November 1st: Start of the excavation season
November 4th: First step discovered
November 25th: Corridor revealed
November 26th: Antechamber discovered and view of
the Annex
November 28th: Access to Burial Chamber and Treasury
November 30th: First press reports about the discoveries
December 27th: First object removed from the
Antechamber

**1000 BCE**

Tutankhamun's Tomb had become so deeply buried
that it was overlooked by the officials who removed
the royal mummies when the Valley of the Kings
was abandoned.

**1151-43 BCE**

Rameses XI chose a site for his tomb only a few yards
from Tutankhamun's. Rubble from the building work
covered the entrance and helped to keep it hidden for
three thousand years.

**1319 BCE**

The tomb is raided by thieves. Carter knew from the
state of the entrance door that it had been broken into
twice in ancient times.

**1323 BCE**

Tutankhamun dies. The pharaoh is laid in his tomb,
surrounded by treasures, and his tomb is decorated. All
chambers and entrances are blocked off. Priests stamped
the door with a seal bearing Tutankhamun's name.

# HISTORY OF ANCIENT EGYPT

The Kingdom of Ancient Egypt lasted for over three thousand years – more than one-and-a-half times as long as the time that separates us form the ancient Romans! To make this huge stretch of time easier to grasp, historians describe it as three long periods of prosperity, with shorter spells of civil war and invasion in between. They call the long periods the Old, Middle and New Kingdoms ("kingdom" in this sense means a period of time, not a realm) and the breaks they call Intermediate Periods. They group the pharaohs in dynasties. A dynasty is a succession of rulers belonging to related families.

The Nile valley was settled in prehistoric times by peoples from surrounding regions who came looking for more fertile land. At first chieftains ruled small areas. These in time came to form two kingdoms—Lower Egypt (the Delta) and Upper Egypt (the south). Egypt's recorded history begins in about 3100 BCE when, according to an old story, the two kingdoms were united by a great warrior called Menes. He became the first pharaoh of all Egypt and built a capital at Memphis.

**2575-2134 BCE** is the time of the Old Kingdom when Egypt is ruled by the third to the sixth dynasties of pharaohs. It is a peaceful period. Huge stone pyramids are built, to provide the pharaohs with everlasting tombs. The most famous are the three at Giza – the Great Pyramid, built c. 2566 BCE for Cheops, a pharaoh of the fourth dynasty, and the pyramids of his son Chephren and of Chephren's successor Mycerinus which stand nearby. The Great Sphinx, an enormous man-headed lion at the approach to Chephren's pyramid, dates from this time too.

**2134-2040 BCE**, the First Intermediate Period. The authority of the pharaohs weakens. Local princes seize the chance to take control. They fight each other to gain power.

**2040-1640 BCE**, the Middle Kingdom—eleventh to thirteenth dynasties. A prince from the city of Thebes reunites the land and a second great age begins. Trade increases, huge marshes are drained, splendid tombs and temples are built and a chain of fortresses is made to keep out envious invaders from the east.

**1640-1532 BCE**, the Second Intermediate Period. Asiatic invaders, called the Hyksos, conquer Lower Egypt. They bring horse-drawn chariots to Egypt.

**1550-1070 BCE**, New Kingdom—eighteenth to twentieth dynasties. The Egyptians of Upper Egypt drive out the Hyksos and reunite the country. The Pharaohs begin overseas conquests, eastwards in Syria and Palestine, and southwards in Nubia. Egypt grows enormously rich, trading in African gold and controlling the mines of Asia. The temples at modern Karnak and Luxor (Thebes) and the great temples cut into the rock at Abu Simbel (in Nubia) are built. The Egyptians have to fight wars with hostile rival powers, especially with the Hittite people of what is now Turkey. Under later, weaker rulers Egypt is attacked by one enemy after another.

**728 BCE** An army from the south puts Nubian pharaohs on the throne.

**661 BCE** The Assyrians capture Memphis and Thebes.

**525 BCE** The Persians become masters of Egypt. The Egyptians hated them most of all.

**332 BCE** Alexander the Great drives out the Persians and puts Greek pharaohs on the throne.

**30 BCE** Egypt becomes a province of the Roman Empire. The old beliefs are forgotten. Temples and palaces fall into ruin and are buried by the sand.

# GLOSSARY

**amulet** charm or piece of jewellery, thought to have magical protective powers.

**Annex** the room attached to Tutankhamun's tomb where treasures were stored.

**anthropoid** shaped like a human.

**burnished** polished by rubbing with a hard smooth tool.

**cache** group of objects hidden underground.

**canopic jars** jars to hold a mummy's internal organs. Early Egyptologists gave the jars this name after the city of Canopus where the god Osiris was worshipped in the form of a human-headed jar, just like many little jars found by the Egyptologists.

**carnelian** semi-precious red or reddish stone. It is a type of quartzite.

**cornice** horizontal moulded band projecting round the top of a structure.

**crook** stick with a curved end, originally used by shepherds.

**djed** an Egyptian symbol for the god Osiris.

**ebony** very hard black wood which the Egyptians imported from Africa to the south of their country.

**embalmer** someone who preserves bodies with oils and spices before burial.

**egyptologist** scholar who specializes in studying ancient Egypt.

**envoy** someone sent on an official mission to a foreign head of government.

**faience** glass-like substance made by fusing powdered quartz.

**fingerstalls** finger coverings.

**flail** instrument with hinged rods that swing from a handle, used to beat people as punishment.

**frieze** horizontal band of either painted or sculpted decoration.

**gesso** mixture of ground chalk and glue put on wood to make the surface suitable for painting or gilding.

**granite** very hard rock formed mostly from the minerals quartz and feldspar.

**hieroglyph** picture sign. These signs represented both objects and sounds and formed the ancient Egyptian alphabet.

**inlaid** surface decorated by embedding another material in it and then smoothing it to give a level surface.

**jasper** opaque semi-precious stone, a type of quartz, red, yellow or brown in color.

**ka** according to the ancient Egyptians, a person's invisible double, born and going through life with them and, if given food and drink, living on after the person's death.

**lapis lazuli** deep blue semi-precious stone.

**Lower Egypt** the land roughly north of the modern city of Cairo up to the great delta of the river Nile and the Mediterranean Sea.

**mud-brick** bricks baked in the sun, not fired in a kiln.

**natron** type of salt found in the ground in different parts of the world, used in the mummification process.

**New Kingdom** see Old Kingdom.

**Nubia** country to the south of ancient Egypt. The land once covered by this ancient kingdom is now split between Egypt and Sudan.

**obsidian** dark, glass-like volcanic rock.

**Old Kingdom** the period 2575 to 2134 BCE when the earliest known pharaohs ruled Egypt. After years of upheaval more pharaohs ruled from 2040 to 1640 BCE, a period called the Middle Kingdom. Then, after another break, pharaohs ruled again from 1550 to 1070 BCE during the period known as the New Kindgom.

**pall** cloth spread over a coffin or tomb.

**papyrus** reed growing in the Nile swamps. The ancient Egyptians made paper from the pith of its stems.

**pectoral** ornament worn on the chest.

**pylon** tower with sloping sides.

**quartzite** rock formed mostly of quartz.

**relief** surface decoration that projects from its background.

**resin** sap that oozes from the trunks of some trees.

**rites** religious ceremonies.

**sarcophagus** coffin made of stone.

**scarab** dung beetle which hatches from eggs laid in dung. Its emergence as if by magic from the dung and its habit of pushing a large ball of dung ahead of it was seen by the Egyptians as representing the sun god emerging from darkness and propelling the sun across the sky.

**shrine** sacred place; also a cupboard-like container for the image of a god.

**shroud** a cloth in which a corpse is wrapped.

**sunk relief** decoration cut into the surface of the object it decorates.

**symbol** object, or shape, which stands for something else. Symbols are used to represent ideas, such as "life" or "love," which cannot be shown in any other way because they are invisible.

**throw-stick** type of boomerang.

**tyet** an Egyptian symbol of the goddess Isis.

**Upper Egypt** the valley of the river Nile from approximately modern Cairo in the north to Aswan in the south.

**veneer** to cover the surface of a wooden object with a thin layer of more decorative wood, or of more valuable material such as ivory or gold.

**wadj** an Egyptian fertility god.

**wedjat** symbol of the left eye of Re.

# INDEX